An Alphabet Pra

My ABC Praise Book

by
Belle Flynn and
Peggy O'Connell, CSJ

PFLAUM
PRESS

This is my book

____

Printed in the United States of America

Illustrations
Catherine Cleary

Design
Evans-Smith & Skubic, Incorporated

Nihil Obstat
James M. Lavin

Imprimatur
+John R. Roach, D.D.
Archbishop of St. Paul-Minneapolis
July 2, 1986

ISBN 0-89837-1114-7
PP200

Dear Parents,

My ABC Praise Book involves children in experiences of praise and thanks through activities of finding and naming. The notes on page 32 suggest ways to use the book with your child.

After a few readings at home, your child will be able to *read* this book without you and take it to church as his or her way to share in the great thank-you prayer of the Eucharist.

Belle and Sister Peggy

TOYS

Thank You, God, for such a nice day,
for my mom and dad,
for my brother and sister,
for Spot and Whiskers,
for all the fun I had today,
for...

an angry alligator attacking an A.

a bashful bear with a bucket in front of a B.

a colorful caterpillar carrying a C.

a dashing dragon dancing with Ds.

an enormous elephant on top of an elegant E.

a freckled frog fishing for an F.

a giddy goose gliding along on a G.

a happy hippo hugging an H.

an inquisitive iguana interested in I’s.

a jolly jackrabbit juggling Js.

a kicking kangaroo kissing a K.

a lazy lion leaning against an L.

a mechanical moose munching on an M.

a nervous nightingale nesting on an N.

orderly opossums upside down on an O.

a perky pink pig pushing a P.

a queenly quail quilting a Q.

a rowdy rooster resting in the middle of an R.

a silly skunk skipping over stones with an S.

a tubby turtle tying a tag to a T.

a uniformed unicorn under a U.

a victorious vulture vacuuming a V.

a wiggly worm wound around a W.

an x-rayed ox with an X inside.

Thank You, God, for You.

Z-Z-Z-Z-Z-Z-Z

Parent & Teacher Notes

What can young children learn about prayer? They live in a world of wonder and curiosity that teems with sensations beyond their ability to comprehend. Their faith during these years is the faith they share with their parents. The stability in their lives is that their parents provide. Their experience of prayer is the bedtime and mealtime prayers they pray with other family members. Children learn to pray by praying.

What is the plan of the book? *My ABC Praise Book* begins and ends with a child and father praying together at bedtime. The child's prayer on page 5 is simple and concrete. The child thanks God for a nice day, for Mom and Dad, brother and sister, and dog and cat. Throughout its middle alphabetical section, *My ABC Praise Book* spills over with illustrations that picture real and imaginary creatures and objects for the child to name. Alliterated words make the text easy for the child to enjoy and remember.

What is the purpose of this prayer book? *My ABC Praise Book* provides parents an at-home and at-church way to help young children learn to pray. Parents can read the book to their children at bedtime and use it as a basis for a short prayertime. As the children hear the book read, they will remember the text and learn the names of animals and objects in each alphabetical illustration.

In addition to this at-home use, *My ABC Praise Book* is a book children can take to church with them. The activities of praising God by naming God's creatures and saying thank you for them are in the spirit of the Eucharist, the Church's great thank-you prayer.

How do parents and teachers use the book? Read *My ABC Praise Book* aloud. As children hear and enjoy the alliterative text repeated, they will remember much of it.

The detailed illustrations are for the purpose of children finding and naming the animals or objects on each page which begin with the letter of the alphabet pictured. Spend time helping your child name what he or she finds on each page. *My ABC Praise Book* encourages a love of words and names for things.

A special creature, a friend of the child who is praying on pages 4-5, appears on each page of the book. Your child will enjoy naming this creature and finding how it participates in the fun of each page.

My ABC Praise Book provides opportunity for children to build skills appropriate to young children's development—finding shapes, naming, identifying letters, enjoying words. The book also builds skills in learning the meaning of such spatial prepositions as *in front of, over, on, under, around, in the middle of, inside, upside down.*

The children's experience of naming creatures and objects in their world and thanking God for them will later grow into understanding of the concepts of praise and prayer.